Can't Hold This Nut Back:

Poems & Thoughts

By - Freeznutz

Cover: "Sirius Arrival" by Fatahma Odebe aka Ananda Free

Copyright ©2024. All Rights Reserved

First Edition

Can't Hold This Nut Back: Poems & Thoughts

ISBN: 978-1-7346262-1-6

Library of Congress Control Number: 2024909602

Praying Hands

Lord cover them with your mercy,
protect them with your grace.
Go with them in places they should not be.
Go before them opening the way for their highest
good,
let your immeasurable love be their portion.

Tears are her language;
the praying mother takes to kneeling,
calling on the unseen to move the unknowable,
to make a way for the fruits of her womb and the
ones of her choosing.

She knows the words of prayer and uses them
ritually.
In a world filled with pitfalls and setbacks, her faith
is a concrete expressway to destiny.
One day the babies will grow, maybe they too will
pray as she does, head bowed, heart lifted,
surrendered.
By example she shows the way,
even if they neglect the path,
her prayers continue to buoy.

Fresh Fruit

The tree withered, after his curses;
could only wonder how growing and being
could bring it to such a tragic end.

"The lifegiver cursed me to die," a crinkled leaf
testified.

A murder pecked the ground nearby.
"Seems the master was in a foul mood."
"I heard he was craving a certain fruit," a crow
cawed.
"Shouldn't he have known it's not the season for
those?" the leaf's weak voice shuddered.
"The master gets what he demands or closes the
door on everyone's plans. That son of man is no
mere man."

The day grew long, birds and beasts retreated to
their places of peace. The dead tree casts no shadow
in the dark. By daylight, not even a witness to the
unimaginable, just sticks breaking, falling to the
ground, dust to dust.

Wild-Child

They're loud and angry
Quiet and compliant
Full of fear and courage
Want and freedom
They need a hug

They turn tape dispensers into guns
Brooms into bats
Belts into whips
Words into bombs
They need our love

They run laughing into the wind
Come back crying with a bruise
They forget everything except
The one time you broke a promise
They need our help

They see beyond the voice
All the way to the heart
They take the time to go deeper
We need their truth

Even the barren woman has a son,
The sterile man a daughter

Each one teach one, not just a cliché

The only way our world will end its assisted suicide
Is when we recognize the child inside
And share with one/some outside

Youthful Vigor . . .

Youthful vigor, pull the trigger.

"Sorry" Can't bring the dead back,
 nigger.

Cold ice walking the block,
now a sack of sobbing sorry,
on a lice infested cot.

Video thugs entice youth to sell drugs;
how many generations lost to money over love?
The game is fast, players race to the track fighting
for a seat.

He was hot on the street,
Now he's cold meat on a slab,
covered with a sheet.
Was it worth it?
The drop-top, the rims, the blood diamonds,
the women?
Ask him.
6 feet under there ain't much shinin'

Youthful vigor, pull the trigger.
"Sorry" Can't bring the dead back,
 nigger.

WAKE UP! Young world!
you're giving it away.
the old adage holds true,
crime doesn't pay.
Unless you invest more in prisons
than educating the youth,
Dope dealer dreams are not bulletproof.

He was a Freshman,
just on the campus for kicks,
not concerned with class,
just slinging green grass and cutting green chicks.
Now he's a statistic,
another brother in a cage, waiting to turn a trick.

Youthful vigor, pull the trigger.
"Sorry" Can't bring the dead back,
Nigger.

MEASURE

How does one measure personal growth?
Those things which once provided succor,
entertainment, excitement, no longer entice. There's
no enjoyment; the intoxicants now repel. A new
level has been reached.

A sense of mourning for the past; it's dead, don't
dig it up in hopes of resurrecting that which has
decayed. There is no joy in dancing with a corpse.
It's time to join the newness of being. Liberated, the
freshness of dispassion flowing without detachment.

This wondrous experience is not to be chased, it's
the reward of being in place. The victory of
embracing there is nothing to win, yet so much that
must be lost; ego, worry, fear, the need to fit in and
be somebody, is all gone. A teardrop for the dead
which once felt so alive but is now of no use.
Freedom is a lonely road, only the fearless tread.

Man in Mirror

My face holds lines it never did before.

is it me in the mirror or a memory,
a projection of what I imagine myself to be?

the clock spins,
no one stops it.
If i could i wouldn't;
the passing itself is joy.

castrate the atomic dick/
free the womb

our tears
are not for our own selves
but for everyone else
who we cannot touch
those whose trauma
makes us immobile
even though we must do something
now

the idiot box is on TV1 and they are not talking
about congo or darfur or burma (or gaza)
rape is not sexy
it's dirty, that grit under our fingernails
we thought
we dug out the last time
it's too messy
sorting through the broken wombs of 7
year old girls and 78
year old grandmothers
piled high in hospitals where
bulletproofed yonis are not under
construction
even though there are guns

piercing wombs
forcing themselves
desecrating life's temples
blasting
the earth to bits
like that damned bomb at Hiroshima
that was just the precursor
to these 21st century atomic dicks

she is reflecting back our
ugly side
if millions of wombs
are being systematically destroyed
by militias
who are hungry for bread and new
uniforms and
perverted profit-seeking CEOs
masturbating with lubricants of instability
then we must
scrub our egos off the mirror
and see that we too are
perpetrating
global wombicide
on ourselves
how careless we have been with our wombs!
sticking
anything and anyone
into our holy sphere
norplant the pill nuvaring

suction-aspiration vacuum abortion
c-sections
scheduled for convenience
bleached tampons
latex condoms
dicks that catch amnesia
as soon as we get pregnant or have a miscarriage
spermicides speculums
vagisil summer's eve
douching apparatuses
we slice up bits of ourselves
daily with ignorance
and wonder
at the abominations leaping across the ocean
in the bushes of afrika
we wonder why the earth is dying
in slow motion
as we assault our wombs for $4.99 a pack at CVS
each month
this cycle there's more blood
caffeinated fibroids
hysterectomies
mastectomies
trapped in underwire bras
thongs spandex
using nair even when it burns
razors
punching holes in the clitoris
for more bling

paper cuts from dollar bills stuffed
between ass cheeks
nicotine addictions
inverted uteruses via stiletto fixations
corsets control top stockings mad cow's milk
corn chips cheetos and caramel when our heart
breaks
again the sugar feeds tumors in the womb
anti-viral drugs that weaken the immune system
mandatory HPV vaccines
because black girls' yonis are still the best lab rats
for gynecology
dildos and vibrators laced with petroleum
generational self hate smeared on with
skin-lighteners
the womb
has been under
duress for a long time

if bands of armed cowards
have been raping women in the pitch black of night
for centuries
then the Womb God
must be indicting all of us
for abusing our wombs
for allowing those who are unworthy
to fuck us
even after they have given us herpes
or lied about fucking over some other womb

for needing him to validate us
for not wanting to be fully responsible
for our wombs
She must want to know
why on earth
we have been too afraid to confront
those who violate us
why we dumb-down our powers waiting on them
to tell us we are beautiful
why we tolerate sexual harassment in order to feed
our families
or verbal abuse because the rent is due
why we ignore our intuition when we don't like its
message
why we are ashamed to heal from
childhood sexual abuse
why we hold onto anger
and haven't forgiven ourselves
why we'd rather feed our babies formula
than breast milk
why we haven't been dancing together
why we have forgotten the songs
why we don't remember which herbs heal what
why we eat
foods that kill us
why we lay on our backs in labor
rather than squatting
why we forget to love ourselves first
the Womb God is crying out

through the screams of the woman raped by soldiers
in front of her children
she is too ashamed to speak out
but what then is our excuse?

we are the ones raped
and the ones raping ourselves
the blood
is on all our hands
gripping cell phones
fingering laptops
manufactured with the mined coltan
that funds war on our wombs
we must castrate the capitalist fallacy
release its suffocation of our indigenous wisdom
expunge its toxins clogging our pores
contaminating our water
polluting our air
making our seeds impotent so that we can't plant
our own food
in our earth
our womb is awaiting the resurrection of
consciousness
the Womb God is holding her ear to the ground
listening out for the voices
declaring love for the womb
celebrating our wombs
knowing the worth of our wombs

but in the flood of our silence
she spins tsunamis erupts volcanoes
sending louder wake-up calls
we are sleepwalking
through the valley
of battered wombs
and it is too late to play dumb
we must reclaim our womb power
now
to be free
to love again

Where's Darryl?

Darryl?
He not coming for recess?
He dead!
Throw the ball!

Lessons in mortality come so quickly in streets
described as
jungles
there's no forgiveness for letting the package
tumble,
falling through eternity
chalk outlines mark finish lines.
it's a miracle so many poets retain the ability to
rhyme
despite empty stomachs and hard times

the only true reality in this matrix comes from those
discarded
with cell blocks and tombstones allotted

why search for the resurrection

when messiahs occupy corners

awaiting upper room conversions
firing up the wrong spirits
doing their best to navigate roads paved in hate
Golgotha awaits

after the Assassination of so many greats
why would anyone wait to scrape the plate?
So many Darryl's dead yet the game continues
hope you set a few records so the future will
remember you

Corny

His one eye should have been the only clue needed, a wrinkled pocket the only evidence of the missing orb. He moved too confidently for someone with an impairment. With long strides he crossed the room in 6 steps, too smoothly, too quickly to plan for an escape.

The bar was crowded for a Tuesday, a dull roar of voices trying to be heard over the rapper on the open mic. Used to be karaoke and poetry, but ever since the record labels came to town everyone was turning to MCing as a path to wealth.

"Nigga! Yo shit's ass!" someone yelled from the crowd. The guy on stage looked damn near 40, his hair braided in rows, falling back from his receding hairline didn't help. He should've worn a hat.

"Git yo bitch ass off the stage Cornell!" It's really bad when old high school classmates recognize you and start heckling.

Someone threw a handful of peanuts, hitting Corny above the eye. Another peanut ricocheted off his forehead, landing in the void in the stranger's face. Cornell exited the stage.

The stranger turned slowly. Silence covered the room as though everyone was seeing this guy for the first time. He locked in on the man who had thrown the nuts. The guy, dressed in his going out best, stumbled getting up, knocking his chair over. Out of habit he reached down to right it when, wham! An open hand at the base of his neck sent him sprawling. He jumped up quickly, his hands ready in a fighting stance. He might as well have been standing with his arms at his side. The stranger hit him with a kick to the side of his head that sent him flying into the rail around the bar. He slumped to the floor wet with spilled drinks and slept.

The stranger pulled a bankroll from his front left pocket, peeled off two $100 bills, placed them on the bar and walked out. The sleeping man's friends rushed to wake him. No one knew who the stranger was, but no one ever clowned Corny again.

The legend was created that Corny was the mastermind of a vicious crew of one-eyed killers. Corny parlayed this myth into a career as a gangster rapper with all the trappings of money, cars, clothes and hoes, or so the story goes.

Feel them...

all around me,
from before aryan raids threw shade over the sun,
their enlightenment a shadow cast from our dark
star long dormant,
these tea-drops make me hiphop past revenge
straight to we are kings and queens again,
to #weareGodsreturn revelations off the pages,
cause my mind's not confined to computer time nor
intelligent design
that's far from divine,
inhaling nanoparticles of sat chit ananda bliss
consciousness,
he's got the whip or world in his hands or rising
from his pores,
Odom is a moor washed ashore to Lilliputian
worship,
praying the mothership cracks the sky soon...its
high noon

BLM

Imagine a people so stripped of all sense of worth, with no anchor, drifting, seeking something, anything to make sense of a world that uses you, yet refuses to see you. Then in a moment when the trauma becomes too much to avoid, the senseless violence of the state is center stage on every screen again and magically the perfect slogan arises from the ether, Black Lives Matter! A rallying cry for everyone, even those who are the subject of the slogan who needed something to believe in. Even after the marches ended, without ending police violence against black people or anyone, ended without justice for many of the victims who sparked the uprising, ended with many of those who took to the streets being charged and convicted of crimes, despite all of the disappointment of fighting a protracted battle and not winning, people walked away with one thing, a slogan, a rallying cry, a meme, Black Lives Matter for which many are willing to kill, mostly metaphorically, as though 3 words are essential to addressing 400+ years of pain.

Clinging to the slogan as though those labeled "black" had forgotten who mattered in attempts to blend in with white culture. Or was it that those words were intended to rewire or even make clear to others that black lives mattered for a moment during the Civil Rights Movement in Alabama, when the adults on the front lines had been beaten and jailed to the point of exhaustion and leadership agreed to allow the children, who kept showing up to participate in the marches, to march officially in the hopes that the earth couldn't stomach seeing young people attacked and abused by rabid racists represented by civilians and state authorities. The horrific scenes of water hoses, dogs and baton beatings shocked the globe, yet the hatred and myths of supremacy which fueled the outbursts of violence didn't end with media coverage.

Here we are almost 60 years later thinking media coverage will do something that only an acid bath, if that, would do. Words, no matter how clever or poignant, are just that. The fact that some are carrying these words as a badge of courage and are willing to attack others who misappropriate the words with expressions such as "white lives matter" or "all lives matter" as though fighting against these words, these ideas, is essential to honoring desecrated humanity.

Who told us words are violence? Words and the correct or incorrect use of them is so essential to achieving a sense of freedom and liberation, where the idea of race is no longer a barrier and systems established in hate and dehumanization are left as a historical memory and warning of how evil humans can be to one another. If only it all could be ended with the right phrasing. Yet this isn't the truth.

Well-meaning people have been conned by a criminal bait and switch. Instead of justice, freedom or reparations, they've been given a slogan. That slogan has come to mean everything and nothing at the same time. Those who didn't know they mattered didn't learn it from a catch phrase. Those in denial of others' humanity didn't suddenly come to a new consciousness. After all these words, though valuable, are nowhere near strong enough or focused on the issue.

Before there was Black Lives Matter, BLM stood for Black Liberation Movement. Those words carried gravitas, a movement, a call for liberation much stronger than one for recognition.

Liberation from what/whom; towards what? A movement from where, to what? These questions sustain generational engagement for change which is required to overcome centuries of white supremacy and racism.

Black Lives Matter is declarative, yet there's an implied, and so what? Black Liberation Movement gave birth to Black Liberation Army, an acknowledgment of the war being waged against black individuals, families and communities. A commitment to no longer just be on defense but also create some offense. Cause how does one fight an armed enemy with picket signs alone?

Our lack of historical memory and analysis has us here again fighting an armed enemy, empowered by the state, with slogans and marching. Knowing in our hearts the battle/war/freedom/liberation can't be won this way. Some hold onto a catch phrase because it's all that's left. They will kill, even metaphorically through tweets, IG posts and defame anyone who doesn't hold the slogan sacred, as some magic spell to open a doorway to Shangri La. It's tragically comic watching victims/survivors of race-based terrorism, fight their counterparts over a 3-word phrase, which magically appeared at the right time in the right place to become more than the moment would allow.

Liberation is not loudly debated or envisioned as a cause. Instead, we choose to fight over an identity which has been established from antiquity. The greatest crime is the world being robbed of the truth that not only do black lives matter, black lives are the foundation of humanity and our collective existence on this planet. This truth, once embraced by so-called black folks, will be the end of any need to appeal for recognition/acknowledgement and will be the beginning of true liberation, which no one can give, which can only be lived and expressed through living/being.

Rocks at Birds

Christs appear periodically to be crucified.
It makes us feel powerful to topple idols,
"He wasn't shit anyway, dusty ass carpenter's son."
Never recognizing the Christ within and that with
each toppled giant we get smaller and smaller.
Cause who would want to shine, just to be told your
light is fake and hurting the eyes of those who'd
rather not be awake?
So we celebrate fallen heroes of our past, forgetting
that their leadership was denied.
When they were alive, they too were crucified.
A ghost is easy to toast, as the Gods walking among
us today are scoffed at and mocked;
"God wouldn't dress like that, talk like that, marry
someone like that."
Still stuck in the judgment seat, as if throwing
stones at birds helps us fly.

FRIYAY

they say happy Friday, the slave way

cause freedom comes when the time clock sings

you liberated to get week until the end

then back at it again

oh, for more happy hours to drown my heart in whiskey sours

oh, I pray for more clubs to pound my headaches away to flashing lights and costumed freaks ready to give a little ghetto heaven right after a stop at 7-11 for protection and maybe a pill to guarantee erection

oh, what a time to be alive

right at 4:45; maybe I'll even sneak out a few minutes before the cock crows to beat the traffic on the road to rage

today is the day

Friyay

DOPE ADDICTS

Infected by meds
Weary, hoping for Big Daddy
To soothe their wounds
Mind addled
Too many conflicting half truths
To build a whole world

Narcissus frozen in a billion shards of glass

Everyone addicted to their own voices
Echoing from palms

Superheroes are long gone
Superegos rule the day

So entertained
the end comes
before the drugs wear off

UPRISE

Rapidly the walls are falling faster than the bricks
flying to replace them,
there will be no rebuilding of these bigoted
barricades, even the superhuman feats attributed to
#freddiegray only pull the shade away from what
we always knew...amerikkka genocide belongs to
you.
You've always killed the young with a steady diet of
hate.
Even immigrants arrive to join the game, though
late.
Stereotypes provide the soundtrack to struggle, but
the tides have turned, and we the people will not be
muzzled.
Guns and tanks you'll bring in force, flash bang
grenades, the charging horse; your loyalists will
defend how much freedom you provide as the
curfew drops and they cower inside.
Those that can see, hear and feel, been known, the
America of fables has been cloned.
Those words penned by slave holding men were
simply a deception behind which to hide their sins.
Now in daylight we're forced to choose the nation
of the anthem or the one we see on the news.

Around the world the red, white and blue stands for bombs, drones, war and the corporations which profit from death, the coalition of the willing intent on killing till neither human nor environment are left.

From the neglected and forgotten rise the last battle cry, "we don't die, we multiply! "

From the mouths of babes songs of freedom erupt, adults of conscience rush to join the chorus, "I'd rather die than be a slave! I'd rather die than be a slave! I'd rather rebel than accept these lies and behave!"

#Uprising #buildbettermodel #NowTime

Love Divine

Ever love someone so much until hurt turns to joy?

Questions answer themselves...time disappears into
moments together,
eternities apart?

Love is divine art painted by hearts
willing to open and flow over life's canvas,
till even the anguish takes on sunset colors,
we cover each other in rounds of salvation.

the cross is a plus sign
you + I = divine
aging like wine,
Intoxicated,
elated

so thankful we let go to let god give us everything
we didn't know how to find

MESSAGE

i had to shoot the message
the messenger long dead
covidxmas this year
santas social distancing
amazon got the contract
to drone my home
the elves been cloned
internet of things hardwired my dreams
had to reset the wifi
more blood on the floor
betta dance
the flames higher than ever

you still wearing leather
thought the vegans would've stabbed you by now
how now brown cow
throw your hands in the air if you breaking your
vows

six in one hand halfa dozen in the other
boy you look just like your mother
the lies boiled till the pot had to pop
and it don't stop
till babylon drop

you still wearing leather
thought the vegans would've stabbed you by now
how now brown cow
throw your hands in the air if you breaking your
vows

the young gathered with signs and sticks
sick of the politrix
their tax dollars fought back with batons and
barriers, masked men in armor ready to rain
chemical death in a pandemic
what a public health plan; blunt force and chemical
war brought to you by every dollar you ever spent
and your elected selected government
and you still out here trynna make rent.
don't take much these days for the troops to hit the
street
they been priming on black lives for 4 centuries
 paddy rollers patrollers, check the volumes of
Tupac
jake was doing dirty in Atlanta and got Pac'd Pac'd

With signs and strollers, democracy is a family
game
they chant his name Floyd Aubrey and hers Breanna
Taylor
there's so many names to chant, FREE PALESTINE

it reads like the book of numbers in and upside
down bible
on a street where tyranny just won a skirmish in the
war for truth and justice
your mind is your musket
from memes to plotting escapes from the scene
didn't expect the burning eyes, constricted throat,
loss of sight,
the people united are a sight

I was rolling with my team just out here speaking
up for the American dream
"No Justice No Peace!"
"Whoose Streets! Our Streets!"
we scream and stand and march and chant and sing
and push,
till the push back comes with batons and boots and
shields and armor and bullets and gas…
this is what voting got me? Not voting got me?
If Covid didn't get me, the tear gas will,
paid my taxes, didn't know chemical gas in the face
came with the bill

LET IT GO

Touch it, feel it, let it go.
legacy is what you do, not what you know.
attached to material life is like holding snow,
wet when it left, for a second it was cold though.
Imagining any of this is more than a dream, until
the curtain falls and the white light hits the screen;
projections, reflections, distracting my attention,
in the race for the divine there are no honorable
mentions.

Touch it, feel it, let it go.
 sticky as an apiary,
optimistic as January,
wishing on a star got your teeth knocked out, under
a pillow waiting for the tooth fairy.
If life is pain, then where's the painkiller?
give me the raw so i can come realer
 there's a crossroad with no christ, in the darkness
one finds the light.
 how does it feel when they all say you're wrong,
until it turns out you're right

Committed to the change.
 calling on the Divine Mother's name.

you want to hold on to the moment but you already
came and now you're drained
like a monkey that's trained, dancing to the cranked
song from a box whose mechanics you don't
understand,
life is an hourglass our dreams running sand

touch it, feel it, let it go…
is the way of eternal man

Got the itch

Under the skin
I feel a creepin'
Give me a hand
Mines just won't reach in
To soothe
The crawling irritation
Need some support
To ease this situation

The jones from my veins
To my bones
The itch I can't scratch
Won't leave me alone
Can you get the doctor on the phone?
Got a botheration, with no end zone.

Rub me, touch me, scratch me
Relieve me
This aggravation refuses to leave me
I need a Savior
With the touch to free me

For the glory…

fights tore my man's hands up,
ten toes down,
letting the world know he's too tough.
His world no bigger than 4 streets and 6 blocks
legend large enough to leave him
caged up.

For the glory,
gridiron heroes
collisions with neither steel encasement nor
seatbelt,
just a simple helmet and face mask.
An amateur career with professional CTE
credentials,
no investigation of his instability to be expected,
statistically predicted
black a synonym for wicked;
threw the ball, caught the ball, ran the ball
gifted.
Crowds gone now,
not even family visits.
He still can't tell you why he did it.
How he got caught up,
to end up,

caged up.

She was so cute,
precocious,
Precious,
attractive
to older fellas.
She paid no attention,
stayed true to her girls,
plans to see the world,
first stop, campus to earn her degree
moved there to study books and theories.
She mastered scams of mastercard and american
express
shopping sprees came too easy and ended quickly.
caught up,
stunting for the gram.
Now she's caged up,
DAMN!

The beast greases the streets
slip away into the pot
another victim of the fiendish plot
to take your soul as your body rots

The beast's so fine in the night until daytime
 when the clock unwinds

the festering flesh and rotted tongue
hold you for an eternal kiss
leaving you numb
the cage drops
like an illusionist trick
you were on a winners run!
where'd the devil come from?

Too late for the glory

Sour Wine

I thought I had forgotten the taste of wine
till you flashed thru my mind
leaving a trail of drunken celebration

it's your laugh
kind of haunting bordering on insanity
you're definitely manic
like a yo-yo

I ride your wave of expression
exhausted at the sight of your quick transition
from here to there, is our love

you shock me with abuse and showers of kindness
I rise and fall to your blows and the hugs that follow

how long can this last?
until one of us has enough?
maybe I'll end up cowering in a puddle of mixed
emotion
or you'll realize that this passenger is too willing a
victim and move on to fresher fields

whatever becomes of this tragedy of love at least we shared this time

On The Rag

Calcified pineal booty gods
chasing CERN magic circles
crashing periodic tables
spirit cooking

pots boiling over
sop it up with big mama cornrows
field hollers echo down the block
yayo!
po-po!

basement dojo thick with crypto smoke
token jackpots spin wheel of unfortunates
daddy's home runs,
nights of stolen baseheads turned green actorvists
climates change like soul train line dances thru the
ages

talking heads mounting platforms
sneaking boys 2 men into dorms
podcast trains delayed
ghosted machines learning the ways of men
x-class flare a step away from flintstone age

don't look up
chicken little in every kettle
precious metal queenpins in formation
such is the state of the nation
this flag chafes

Data overload

AI fried
The devil lied
Job complete
Separated you from the soil
The rooted soul
Watch pestilence, privation and boils
Terror throughout the land
Cause one foolishly followed that man
Who only knew to kill, steal and destroy
All his promises mere decoys
Even a win in his game is ultimately a loss
As you stand naked and afraid before the
Final Boss
Before the machine screams
To a shuddering halt
Just admit it was all your fault
To imagine the beast would grant a life of ease
As though there'd be a greater Utopia
Than sweet mango trees
Fields of grains
Cool running waters ease
All pains

We denied all this in exchange for chemical flowing
faucets and

Energy drains
There's still time left
To embrace the divine
Dig into the soil
Reconnect with time
As long as they have yet to block the sunshine
We can be rays of the divine
In a moment
when we turn away from the hamster wheel and
their market plays
the rhythm of eternity awaits
with plenty of space
for us to dance and play

Men at Tables

Men at tables
Calculate
How many must die
To achieve goals
"Only the future will understand"
They say.

Men at tables
Calculate
How much of a disease
Virus to mix with another
Accelerant
To make the perfect contagion
One that can kill
With greatest efficiency or pain
They study science
Build superbugs
"To protect the future
Who will understand,"
Or so
They say.

Men at tables
Create
Programs to calculate
The worth of other men
Women, children
Based on values created by
Men at tables
Pretending
They work for a future
Only they can
Understand....

America Tis of Thee

America is an idea, a creed,
a need to believe that slavers can write freedom into reality
that the white minority is some deity
able to plant seeds of change from sea to shining sea

America is a wedding reception after the vows are splintered
the groom fucking the bridesmaids, the bride the groomsmen
dancing on full condoms
pretending they're all virgins

America is an outhouse pretending to be an ensuite

America is beyond meat, though bloody shoes
betray her lust for life,
Young hearts pump hot on serrated knives,
it's all jive
jazz born from blues,
the moans from Slave row drowned out by banjos

America is the mother you'll never know

she left her sticky infant on the porch to run off with
the preacher's son
full of fire brimstone and bullshit

America would love to be a pimp
but she's a $2 hoe
soon everyone will know she burns you good
from the asphalt to the backwoods

To my forever love

Thinking of you and love as the same
all-encompassing experience of warmth, peace and
joy. From the moment you wrapped me in your
arms,
I've been safe.
Even as you showed me your anger, the love peaked
thru and I saw you as goddess,
divinity gifted to me from eternity…
mother of three mama to many,
your smile lights up any room,
your joy electric
and I get to hold you, kiss you as lovers and be
father to the bright lights you birthed!
some say love hurts and we've been through that.
now we know love heals and
feels all kinds of good

Hip hop is...

the fruit of a planted seed born from neglect and
greed,
as the grandchildren of the dispossessed gathered
capitalism's detritus to paint and beat,
make a pathway to share their day to day,
till all the world could share a common poetic
expression of passion, triumph, pain, resilience.
Against all odds this art shines through as a
reflection of what's aspirational and true,
from the darkest fantasies of death and revenge to
anthems of abiding love between partners and
friends,
legends have emerged from turntables and spoken
word,
gravity defying, body bending, spray painting,
mundane transforming culture,
with the undeniable force of
love, Peace, unity and having fun...
HipHop makes the world one

After Life

Obsessed with preserving the flesh
trying to out-science their fear of death…
with no spiritual connect, just prolonging the truth
there's life after breath

Let Go...

As an instrument the notes played are not your own.

Let go and let god is an aphorism, a one-line love
letter from the divine, the almighty, the one
generator-operator-destroyer, to anyone all willing
to test it. Believing is easy, requires no effort.
The word "life" is testing, failing, learning, testing,
failing, learning, surrendering...
let go and know god is in control, which means I'm
not. I'm the witness, participant and with intention
co-creator of activity experience.

Let go and let god.
Do you even have faith to know that where you are
is where god is?
Not far to go when you let...

LOVE

Love is both pressure and release,
war and peace, knowing and ignorance.
The fragrance that lingers well after the flower has
wilted.

Love gives without end, thus getting everything.

Love is looking at the night sky as stars send light
from beyond simple measures, just to let me know I
am not alone.

Love is the 1001 questions of a child and the tireless
answers of the questioned adult.

Love is no one's fault, yet everyone's responsibility;
the most pleasurable heavy lifting, an effortless
happening, just delightful and confusing.

Hidden Hand

Thrift store shoplifting
the unforgivable forgotten
back there where history morphs into myth
who left these gifts?
factory rejects
soul music turned ratchet revelries
savage enough to be numbered.
Who imagined it could end any differently with its
origins in slavery?
Before Columbus came, they arrived with charity
and community.
Then Conquest, the dalliance of egoic charlatans
feigning supreme,
like the American dream of Mickey Mouse ears and
climate change,
from home to car to office and back,
imagine the world has a thermostat,
who would you trust to control that?

Black Mirror Traps

On the line between profane and divine
whose hook caught the biggest fish of the Piscean
age? Dead Christ's line history books, just turn the
page. master the keys to being the greatest slave.
masters obscured the world we hardly know, blindly
seeking to find the path, quickly filled with blowing
snow.
where does the time go, as the mind races to keep
pace with designers of mazes and cameras to ensure
all faces have cases?
may have to put the black mirror down and
get back to basics

Meditation

A touch of heaven
the quietude of the moment
infinite depth
falling back into the mother's arms
eternity a breathless away

Jesus Sandals

I bust in with no introduction
to change the world is an act of seduction
by the time you hear the sound there's been an
eruption
you've been weaned on lies and corruption

straight out the gate all love no hate
Aum brings it home
no need to lay prostrate

we are gods return
eternity uncloaked
knowledge of self is more powerful than dope
truth is not hope, it's faith
which knows the value of self
giving value to clothes and all of those shiny
tangibles with catchy handles
can't hold a match to your spiritual candle

thieves in the temple? just vandals
who ramble
debating the straps on Jesus sandals

where we run there's no fatigue
when we feast there's no greed

the way we love there's no fear to impede
we're free and
no proclamation can emancipate we who are god
seed out the gate
politrix can't decide our fate
we are new wine from old grapes
they forgot to calculate

The Great Grift

The supreme leader scheme undermining the
American dream,
waiting for heroic overcomers who articulately
dissect complex historical issues to 15 second sound
bites, dazzling under bright lights.

"Mr President," the huddled masses of media
classes hurl queries as s/he/they saunter away
ducking and waving under helicopter blades. Soon
to be in a secure location, working hard on vacation.
This elimination of accountability as part of the
24-hour news vivisection, leaving the polity a
corpse picked clean, as policy rides the greased
wheels of corporate insiders, trading on
congressional hearing breadcrumbs, often whole
loafs, odds better than Vegas, nothing to lose but the
treasury.

Elections secured by contracts keeping the powerful
back home fed, its true there's nothing to see but
gay sex by the most popular former potus, like
Pilate they threw him on the pyre for the rest of us,
grift or bust.

Risen from the dead

Re-birthday
set apart
not many can say they went there and didn't stay.

now a manchild again

Do you play or get all serious about legacy and
showing up strong?

Even the centenarian says life is not long.

Here it is another new year for you…new you?

Possibly, you broke through to the other side…
AD did that and came back,
painted his room red&black.

i hope you smile,
embracing candlelit moments before
the winds blow…
any wishes left?

Sexy? Not So Much

Everything I know about SexyyRed I learned against my will. The rapper's meteoric rise on biological lyrics like, "my pussy pink my booty hole brown" has her on magazine covers, award shows and all up and down the timeline. The self-professed "raw dog queen" caught a stray recently with the leak of her being sexed.

Now I'm sure there'll be plenty of think pieces about consent, online sleuthing about who leaked it and who the dick belongs to, but what I want to talk about is the wack sex! The dry humping requiring spit to get things lubricated was a clear sign of too little foreplay. The corpse pose spoke to Sexxy's lack of engagement. All I could feel was embarrassment for her and sadness that this is an example of the sex many people are having.

Sex is wasted on the young. The intimacy and vulnerability it takes to really make love requires maturity and experience. The tenderness to take the time to get your partner fully aroused. The interest in them to learn what turns them on and the patience to not put one's own pleasure first, are learned over time. Sadly, most of us learn about sex from porn. A totally fake environment focused on explosive orgasms and as little communication as possible.

There are many comments about Sexyy's video, from critiques of the man's dick size to the juvenile "it ain't pink like you say". My only comment is that she and all women deserve better. Learn about your anatomy and what gets you aroused and teach your partner. Don't have these guys or others ramming all up in you thinking they moving mountains when you're not even wet, let alone aroused from head to toe. This is a teachable moment! 80% of women don't orgasm from intercourse alone. Put the porn down and pick up Mantauk Chia's Multiorgasmic male and female. Take a note from the playground Sexyyred, "don't talk about it, be about it!" Cause the video exposes it ain't all you saying it is ●

Death Cults

Mythology got folks in a death grip...
what type of god puts a plan(et) in motion
where all his followers are waiting for the
apocalypse?

Middle East Messianics

Nobody wins when the family feuds...
all fruits spoiling from one common seed,
cause as Christ exemplified,
the priesthood is corrupt and won't hesitate to make
the peacemakers bleed.

Turkey Time

Of turkeys... This season of giving, when the forgotten are remembered for the fleeting pleasure of guilt relieved. The closing quarter of the year, when corporations give, so they may receive forgiveness at tax time. Those who are on the serving end of the spoon, line up to accept crumbs from the table. Many in need find more solace in pride than in accepting an offering from scoundrels. No, not all who give are bad. There are many who recognize the opportunity presented by a season set aside for sharing. Yet they miss the systemic inequality whose harvest suffers in ill-equipped schools and underpaid labor.

To end the soup line, the turkey offering, the bemoaning of the fate of "others" requires us to see ourselves in the position of those we propose to help. We too are weak and in need of assistance. Somewhere a calling goes unheard, passions have been curbed to the demands of practicality, change exchanged for the disguise of a glove covering the calloused hand. The turkey no longer serves the need of giver or recipient. Even with bellies full, we hunger for the fulfillment of our humanity. Those who offer charity, where do they disappear once the occasion is done? Why do they not extend their giving beyond the exchange of things, to the sharing of their very souls? What type of world finds this acceptable?

We propose to do what many have attempted, address the needs of the marginalized whose suffering has been stereotyped and become a caricature of ineptitude. After generations of abuse and neglect, after hundreds of programs designed to meet the perceived need, cynicism is as good a refuge as anger. One allows for objective distance the other may lead to rash reaction, both allow for the continuance of the status quo. To throw a shoe into the cogs of the machine, to allow daylight to pierce the slave quarters, to allow dreams of freedom to mature into realities of well-tooled responsibility, this is the continued legacy of those who champion freedom.

The mission is to open our hearts, to connect to the open hearts of those around us. This may not end poverty, but what is prosperity other than people sharing in loving exchange with all that is around, encompassing the environment, whether natural or artificial, the creatures and those others who seem so different yet are truly flesh, blood, breath and

bone as we. Such sharing may begin with a holiday
turkey, but it must not end there.

Of turkeys...
give thanks for giving and receiving
this temporary opening,
spanning the distance between
need and have

if only this dance were to last
for more than a season;
if only we were as generous with our time
as we are with our non-perishables;
if only we owned the belief in freedom
Enough to remove barriers to its expression.
the myopia of markets blinds us to the needs of
humanity,
which remains a plant,
thirsty and unprotected from the winds
of politics.

so, we choose a space to operate
fertilize, water, weed and watch
waiting for fruits
bearing testament to the utility of our commitment.
How many trees comprise a forest?

How many seeds must we nurture to make turkey
lines obsolete?
These are questions of accounting not gardening....

Get in Where You Fit In

Transported to another world of masks and men
pretending that dreams deferred is a strategy for
success,
heads bowed to ward off the cold and pay fealty to
the god of their choosing; paper, plastic, binary
devices, wedded to direct deposits, praying
catastrophic seismic events don't portend divorce,
bust down to the simple life of subsistence, a viral
strain of humility must be warded off with stiff
upper lips.

They all lying, we all laying,
revolution the background music playing,
Unable to focus
dial in more distractions,
add a dose of christ killing,
build and destroy idols,
no one remembers when the fight started,
all in for it not to end,
only nature can stop the doomsday clock.

Next?

Reckless youth get shot down,
too far ahead,
the prophet bleeds eternal.

There will be no more Malcolms.
The system recalibrated, lips won't form biting
truths, traded for eloquent acceptance,
the call for black power shifted
to a declaration of value…
we matter?

Our power diluted, our vision sniped,
official genocide policy,
blinded by white Christ zeitgeist.
time to change the day,
we are not to be slaves,
vision anew,
enough schisms to break vesey's resolve,
nat turner we need,
Prophet's bleed.

I AM A LIGHT BEAM -----SCREAM

Kinetic energy moves me to release the seal of
centuries of patriarchy
we are free
the Goddess has risen
no more prison of conformity confusion doubt
no longer dumbed down we rise up
enlightened by this ray of love

I AM A LIGHT BEAM -----SCREAM

Touch the core of being still
flowers bloom from this tender heart
hear the vibration of eternal celebration
peace is the prayer answered as Grace
turn to face the mirror of the Master within

I AM A LIGHT BEAM -----SCREAM

Drop all weights
take flight on wings of love
uncovered unfettered unashamed
no longer a player in the game
I am the blue flame, the violet light, the darkest
night
mysterious deep and rich

connect with this simplest truth, timeless youth
breathe deep and know we are one light of the Sun

I AM A LIGHT BEAM -----SCREAM

Closing Hours

"It is still not clear who will replace the US
consumer as a source of demand." World Bank
President Robert Zoellick warned Monday that
many risks still exist on the road of recovery as the
world economy is "in a precarious state." Yes
indeed, the tide is turning, tsunamis rising, deep
beneath the earth feel the quaking, sleeping dogs
awakening, realizing their names have been taken in
vain to create global pain.

money maneuvers,
masked mass murder under freedom's flag,
bombs over Bhagdad,
drones and clones,
so afraid in the land of the free,
folks don't even leave home, except to rush to the
grinding stone,
spreading tumors by cell phone,
obese on food that's fast,
mentally emaciated underclass,
wishing for green grass, actually chem-lawn
sprayed, again we've been played!
to what do we owe this dishonor?
To which direction do we pray?

In the arms of pharmaceuticals we run away --
the need for healthcare may outpace the greed called
corporate welfare, if the people can be persuaded
that it's worth it to care --
we do matter when we see the mad hatter is simply
mad and needs to be captured under the looking
glass,
where the light of day will fry his vampire ass --
still teaching Columbus colonized the Indians in
history class,
no truth to be found in the halls of matriculation,
evolution is born anew at sunrise after a dreamy
gestation
what do you see behind closed eyes?

if it's not liberation, then enjoy the daily dose of
lies,
news to keep the mind on snews,
steady regurgitation of emotional abuse

Enviro-mental

Last drop of oil, Last gasp of air, not even enough for a prayer...How many species must die so my car can go? How many wetlands turned to oily wastelands for the sake of convenient transportation? In a nation built on slavery and genocide, who feels a pinch when filling up the ride? So separate from cause and effect, we wonder if we need to slow down after the wreck. Business as usual, profits at all costs, discounting 7 generations or more, smiling on the way to the mega-store, constantly extracting with no way to give back. No intent to return what's been taken from the ground and burned, no reciprocity to the support of our humanity lost in the insanity of unlimited growth fueled by vanity.

What are we without fresh water, fertile earth & clean air? If we can't sustain life here, it's hubris to think we'll do better elsewhere. There's no security in oil, more disasters than we care to admit. The corporation is the gun, greed the bullet, we the people squeeze the trigger, making decisions oblivious of consequences. The dead children of Operation Iraqi Liberation (oil), afghani-pipeline-istan, Nigeria fields awash with crude hued blood, strange fruits from Alberta tar sands, oil mixed with mud. We have found the enemy and he is me, i must embrace the other, make the criminal my brother, unconditional love like the fully engaged mother, then we transform pain into joy, blame into opportunity, our oily reality into a sun-drenched, windblown future of sustainability.

Full Metal Mental

What are killer's made of?
Basic training reduces complex men to basic
instincts of kill or be killed -- there's no time to ask
questions, just follow orders. The training is that
good. Until some take the training a little too
serious and start painting outside the lines; then the
powers that be start whispering "war crimes," as
though war in and of itself isn't a crime; destroying
landscapes, the psychological damage akin to
cultural rape.

Who's the hero when killing is wholesale and
civilians are counted as collateral? We all die a
little, while some line their casket in cash. Why do
we insist on war as the path to change? What to do
with warriors who have learned that killing is the
game? Let them back into the family though things
have changed? Some burn slow inside, some blow
up and let bullets fly. Abroad it can be overlooked,
years later investigations and confessions in books.
Too bad death gives no second looks. In the heat of
battle men lose their minds, we blame the product
but not the manufacturer; the soldier not the general

nor policy maker; those who train to hate continue,
as we castigate the hater.

Seat at the Table

The crowd flowed into the basement cafeteria.
Hosts stood in 3 sections, fingers held up, signing
seat availability. They came. You may call them
homeless or dispossessed. I see them as the
wandering parts of us, our consciousness denied;
the playful child who never wanted to sit still, just
wanted to run and play and laugh and tell stories,
throw rocks, climb trees, skip and dodge and be.
The philosopher with no degree. Refuse tossed
aside by military and penitentiary. We, who find
shelter in bottles and libraries.

There he is at a table of 6, enjoying the leftovers of
our scheduled lives, restaurant wastes of our haste
to build more than we can take. Here she comes, a
queen. Her thrown glances indict us for allowing a
family to carry their world in bags from cave to
cave in these modern days. She knows the machine
has a ghost cause it died so long ago, rusted like
american manufacturing, know-how and freedom.

Are you crying, again? Like you did when you saw
me on t.v. covered in flies, belly full of worms and
gas. Call me neighbor and save that water for a

garden. We fools believe we're wise, chasing dreams advertised. The awakened are criticized for revealing the dream is cancerous inside. A little more soup for the road, keep it stirred so no one will know so many pieces make up the mix, we all have a part in this cabaret.

Shift change. Glad you came, now drift away. Sure to see you again, transient friend invisible (but for the hours we shared today) until we no longer look away. Be Happy (the alternatives just can't compete :)

Writing On the Wall

jesus wrote the message on the wall;
damn, these niggas can't read.

jesus fed thousands with a couple croakers,
one trout and a loaf of day old wonder bread;
the people asked for hot sauce.

jesus gave his blood,
the people drank it like wine.
too drunk to realize the sacrifice;
the people wore the tools of his death as ornaments.

Jesus came back,
No one recognized him.
He was cool with that.

Made in United States
Orlando, FL
06 December 2024

54515257R00054